A Closer Look at Ariel

A Closer Look at Ariel

a memory of Sylvia Plath

by Nancy Hunter Steiner
Afterword by George Stade

Faber and Faber

London · Boston

First published in Great Britain in 1974
by Faber and Faber Limited
3 Queen Square London WC1
Reprinted 1974
Reprinted 1976
Reprinted 1978
Printed in Great Britain by
Unwin Brothers Limited
The Gresham Press, Old Woking, Surrey
All rights reserved
ISBN 0 571 10492 4
(Faber Paperbacks)
ISBN 0 571 10491 6
(hard bound edition)

Extracts from Sylvia Plath's work are included by kind permission of Miss Olwyn Hughes

To my father,
and to other fathers,
other daughters . . .

A memory of Sylvia Plath

Although her work suggests that she was a deeply troubled young woman, casual acquaintances have often described Sylvia Plath as bright, creative, pleasant, and otherwise unexceptional. That such a paradox exists is a clue to Sylvia's nature. As her roommate from 1954 to 1955, the critical period just after her first suicide attempt, I was acutely aware of this duality. Even so, I can relate only a fragment of Sylvia's story, one of many such fragments that her biographers will someday weave together into a definitive account that will delineate the woman, the poet, and the work. I can offer only one set of impressions, one slim catalog of events: a vignette that catches Sylvia midway between youth and maturity and suspends her there, in the limbo of memory. Although I knew Sylvia briefly, I knew her well, with the special urgency and sudden familiarity that characterize school-girl friendships. Breaking out of cramped adolescent cocoons, we found ourselves temporarily allied in a metamorphosis that we could neither control nor escape. My memories of her are sometimes warm and loving and sometimes troubling. At its best our friendship was a happy, intimate interlude during which we wore each other like a pair of matching talismans. At its worst, it took on the dimensions of a Passion Play in which I was unwittingly cast as Judas.

The drama took place in a setting that was both remarkable and prosaic. In 1954, Smith College was a reflection of the society that nurtured and supported it. Its student body was part of the anomaly called "The Silent Generation," with the significant difference that this particular student body was exclusively female. No single generalization can capture the unique pattern of influences that came together on that campus at that particular point in time. However, certain observations are too compelling to resist, because they define the preoccupations and proclivities of the undergraduate community into which Sylvia matriculated as a freshman in 1950 and to which she returned in 1954 after the widely publicized suicide attempt and the subsequent emotional rehabilitation which she describes in *The Bell Jar*.

The generation to which we both belonged spent its formative years listening to radio newscasts from the battlefronts of the Second World War—the one that would end all wars. Those years were a time of new opportunities, new fortunes, and new dimensions for the American Dream. We watched as our mothers went off to work in unprecedented numbers, as the nation achieved unparalleled prosperity, and as the people of this country united in unquestioning devotion to a single national cause. We thrived on a diet of tuna fish and macaroni and discovered, when we were old enough to wear silk stockings, that they had all been turned into parachutes. We grew accustomed to sacrifice. When the war ended, we listened in numbing disbelief to tales of Hitler's nearly successful attempt to exterminate the Jews and learned to

10

live with the realities of Cold War and atomic capability. Most of us remained sanguine; if we could not look outward without shuddering, we would turn our gaze inward, instead. Korea was a dark shadow hanging over the boys we knew, but we girls raced off to colleges and universities without them. Dwight Eisenhower was in the White House, and if Joe McCarthy was in the Senate, building a career on accusation and innuendo, what had that to do with us? We had been encouraged since childhood to believe that all would soon be well in the best of possible places and we had no reason, now, to abandon our optimism. We packed our cashmere sweaters and our unshakable convictions in a set of brand-new luggage and were on our way.

In some ways we resembled every generation of undergraduates that has ever assaulted the nation's campuses. We were scrubbed, shining, and expectant. Those of us who chose Smith were no exception. The stereotyped Smith girl of the mid 1950's was a conformist, like thousands of undergraduates there and elsewhere, before and since. She was eager to be recognized as a college girl and she was careful to wear the proper uniform, in this case Bermuda shorts, knee socks, and button-down-collar shirt. Her hair was casually but precisely styled. If possible, she was bony, angular, and flat chested. If not, she devoted a portion of her limitless energy to achieving the ideal: an understated, studied informality that suggested warmth and approachability. She was a doer, busily directing the activities of some prominent or obscure organization in preparation for a future role as a participating member of her community. There was about her an air of noblesse oblige, although in this case it was not necessarily nobility that posed the obligation; in part, at least, it was the type of education she was receiving: an education that placed a high value on involvement. She represented the many levels of the middle class; she was bright, sophisticated, curious, and malleable. She did not seem to resent the mold from which she had been fashioned or the fact that she was interchangeable with dozens of others just like her.

In contrast with this conforming majority the non-conformists were particularly visible. A small coterie of avant-garde beatniks rejected the polish, the costume, and the aspirations of the conformists. This group was especially evident in the scholarship houses, like Lawrence, where girls who needed further financial help agreed to do certain domestic chores in return for a reduction in room and board rates. Many of these girls affected dirty jeans, bare feet, and deliberate gaucheries to demonstrate their contempt for values they considered superficial. They were serious scholars or artists or political activists and they adopted a kind of sartorial asceticism as a means of advertising their individuality. Some of them were honestly not concerned with clothes, social life, or campus politics. Others appeared to believe that wearing a matching skirt and sweater was a form of anti-intellectualism or that because they were "scholarship girls" they ought to look the part. Still others were clearly individuals who were most comfortable doing what they wanted to do, unaware of or unaffected by societal pressure.

Although at first I was not aware of the distinction, I later realized that Lawrence House possessed a particular mystique and was not a cross section of campus attitudes and concerns. Because all of us in Lawrence were at Smith on scholarships and because the possibility of remaining there without them was remote, we brought to even the most trivial activity an almost savage industriousness—a clenched-teeth determination to succeed that emanated from us like cheap perfume. We never stopped being students; we viewed even our diversions as an extension of the curriculum, which could be prodded to provide another perception or another fact to add to our individual arsenals. We were never quite certain when we would be called upon to defend the superiority others had convinced us we possessed, and we amassed a collection of straight A's and superior recommendations to serve as our weapons.

Despite our zealous determination to use education as a stepping stone to wherever it was we were going, we were not particularly competitive among ourselves. The horizons we aimed for did not appear crowded and the meritocracy we pictured was vast enough to provide opportunities for anyone who could meet the entrance requirements. Behind the aging, ivied walls of Lawrence House we developed a surprising esprit de corps, sharing information about courses, study habits, and examination techniques, taking the underclassmen under our experienced wings to help them acquire the tools of academic success. We must have seemed a strange, intense, formidable phenomenon to the girls from other houses who came frequently to visit.

Whatever our individual differences, whatever private forces drove us into opposing segments of the undergraduate population, all of us at Smith shared, I think, a common if hazy sense of the uniqueness of Smith. In spite of its curfews and the crew of doughty Kingsmen who guarded its portals like an army of doting surrogate fathers, Smith was a place where women were regarded as first-class citizens, thoughtful, responsible, capable human beings who deserved the finest faculty, library, and academic environment that a college could provide. That confidence buoyed and sustained us through the thousand pressures and crises which were an inevitable part of the atmosphere. In most cases, it brought forth our best efforts; as the guardians of a remarkable trust we felt a gnawing, sometimes consuming responsibility to prove that it was not misplaced.

When I transferred to Smith for my junior year and moved into Lawrence House I was given a freshman roommate who seemed determined to flunk out as quickly as possible. When the arrangement proved unsatisfactory I asked to be moved to another room. Another room was available, and after some hesitation the housemother agreed that I could move into it. The room would have been Sylvia's if the suicide attempt had not delayed her return. It had not been reassigned, either out of the respect for her image that had already begun to spring up or out of anticipation of her eventual return. No one who had known her appeared eager to occupy the room, even though it was one of the largest and most ideally situated in the house. It was on the second floor and was obviously an upperclassman's room—half of a suite of two identical bedrooms that could be reached from the hall outside only through a common vestibule. The vestibule contained two enormous closets and acted as a buffer against the noise and confusion of the hallway. It was an ideal room for studying and it offered a pleasant view of the library and the assortment of residence houses that were ranged around it in haphazard fashion.

If Sylvia could not exactly haunt the room during her absence, she clearly made her presence felt. She was a frequent topic of conversation in the house; as the months passed I grew familiar with the details of the Plath legend through the speculative gossip that raged at the mention of her name. I knew that she had already established a literary reputation and that she was an outstanding student who had been elected to Phi Beta Kappa in her junior year. I knew also that her attempted suicide had come as a shock to everyone who knew her and I sensed that she was someone very extraordinary, even for Lawrence House. For me, however, no inhibiting memories existed. I was delighted to share the suite with Sylvia's intended roommate, a senior whom I liked very much. I moved in eagerly, not knowing that I would also be compelled into Sylvia's life.

The news of her imminent return to Smith several months later, after a period of psychiatric rehabilitation at a private clinic near Boston, provoked a flurry of conjecture. My curiosity aroused by the bits and pieces of description I had absorbed, I formed a mental picture of this girl-genius whose room I had usurped. Without any hesitation I placed her in the nonconforming minority in the house and on the Smith campus—the group that eschewed the cosmetic trappings in favor of a no-nonsense dedication to their work. I expected her to be a maverick or a rebel and pictured her as plain or dull or deliberately dowdy, a girl who rejected all frivolity in the pursuit of academic and literary excellence. I could not have been more mistaken.

For Sylvia's first meal back in the Lawrence House dining room, the housemother carefully selected the six girls who would be seated at the table with her. She chose girls who could be depended on not to gawk or ask embarrassing questions or lapse into self-conscious silence. For some reason I was included. I remember that I was a few seconds late for lunch; as I hurried across the crowded dining room I noticed the jaunty floral bouquets that graced each table, put there, no doubt, as a cheerful tribute to Sylvia's homecoming as well as a reminder of the gracious life style to which we were all supposedly dedicated. I could see the other girls arranged impatiently behind their chairs, waiting for me to arrive so they could be seated. I could also see Sylvia, and her appearance was so unlike what I had expected that I blurted out my surprise as I reached the table, even before we had been introduced.

"They didn't tell me you were beautiful," I protested.

The other girls shrieked at the impropriety of my remark and Sylvia laughed, too, although I had intended the observation seriously. Nothing in Sylvia's appearance suggested that she was an exception to the prevalent stereotype, and I was amazed that the legend had not included this obviously significant fact. Her clothes and manner seemed deliberately cultivated to disguise any distinction. She did not project any rebellious desire to appear different or to accent her intellectual superiority by wearing it as her only ornament. Her photographs are misleading; Sylvia was a remarkably attractive young woman. She was impressively tall, almost statuesque, and she carried the height with an air of easy assurance. Her yellow hair, which had been lightened several shades from its natural light brown, was shoulder length and had been carefully trained to dip with a precise and provocative flourish over her left eyebrow. Her eyes were very dark, deeply set under heavy lids that give them a brooding quality in many of her photographs. Her cheekbones were high and pronounced, their prominence exaggerated by the faint, irregular brown scar that was the only physical reminder of the suicide attempt. The face was angular and its features strong, a fact that may explain the dark shadows that seem to haunt it in photographs.

She was given a room on the second floor near our suite—a single room that had suddenly become available. She came to our suite often; it seemed natural that she should be there, with her intended roommate, in the room that was to have been hers. Our friendship developed during those visits and we agreed to be roommates the following year, with Sylvia moving into the room that would be empty when my roommate graduated.

We were drawn together by mutual interests and shared pleasures, as well as by the obvious parallel in our furious attempts to appear well rounded. We both seemed determined that no one was going to guess we were "scholarship girls" if, with a little ingenuity, we could appear to belong in the mainstream of campus life. Sylvia seemed particularly intrigued by the many ways we complemented each other. She announced, with mock seriousness, that my Irish coloring was an appropriate foil for her German blondness and that, while I was not as tall as she, I was tall enough to be considered an equal. She

17

referred to me in letters to her mother as her alter ego and often remarked that we presented a mirror image or represented opposite sides of the same coin. She was fascinated by the idea that qualities that were dominant in her personality were subordinate in mine, and vice versa. Although I came to depend on her leadership in many areas, she in turn found resources in me to draw upon. In general, she provided the ideas and the creative imagination; I was a filter through which the inspiration passed, qualifying and tempering what she initiated. She was pleased by the neatness of the alliance and suggested that our combined strengths created an impenetrable fortress—that together we were invincible. I did not understand at the time that alone Sylvia felt defenseless and imperiled.

It is impossible to describe Sylvia in terms that are crisply black or white; she hovered in between, among what she herself called "all those delicious shades of grey." Contemporary accounts often described her as cool, aloof, or distant, but they were describing only the façade—the barricade that Sylvia erected so that she herself could decide the quality and duration of her relationships. To those who knew her well she was warm, direct, and vulnerable. My first impressions, however, confirmed what seemed to be the majority opinion—that except for the penetrating intelligence and the extraordinary poetic talent she could have been an airline stewardess or the ingenuous heroine of a B movie. She did not appear tortured or alienated; at times it was difficult for me to believe that she had ever felt a self-destructive impulse. She seemed eager to create the impression of the typical American girl, the product of a hundred years of middle-class propriety. She actively disliked the little band of rebels in the house. Their bare feet, rude manners, and coarse language offended her.

Although our generation had not yet defined "The Establishment" or identified its shortcomings, Sylvia and I shared a conscious need to work within it, to act in a way that would bring credit and pride to those who had championed us. We expected people to act rationally and predictably and we demanded compliance from ourselves as well, although, like most adolescents, we were capable of enormous self-deception to excuse our departures from what we considered appropriate behavior. We might privately criticize the code that had shaped us and the anachronistic irrelevance of its prohibitions, but we possessed a deeply conditioned respect for authority and little inclination to act out our restiveness.

While outwardly playing the serene undergraduate, Syl was writing poetry in which the circumstances were not so neatly arranged. In her work, ugly, distorted worlds exploded and erupted in metaphoric profusion. The paradox troubled me at first; later I could guess at some possible explanations. Sylvia constructed images as an engineer designs a bridge—with painstaking, almost mathematical attention to every detail. She wrote slowly, plodding through dictionary and thesaurus searching for the exact word to create the poetic impression she intended. Sometimes she chose words with disquieting connotations for their shock value. Often, however, the poetry reflected the turbulent process that was taking place beneath her placid exterior. At her core, Sylvia experienced a welter of raging emotions and violent impulses, and on the surface, to keep them in check, she wore the mantle of a bourgeois lady, as inhibiting and restraining as a straight jacket. The words did not flow in a steady, effortless stream. They could be released only painfully, bit by agonizing bit, as though wrenched free of some massive blockage.

She was introspective and eager to talk about herself, the suicide attempt, and the events that led up to it. She described the previous summer as a series of frustrations. A brief expedition into the New York world of fashion journalism triggered a spiraling depression from which she could not extricate herself as the summer wore on. What should have been a stimulating, exciting round of gala festivities produced only a mounting tedium that did not subside even at the chance to meet and interview outstanding figures in the literary world. She found the work artificial and banal. She tried several other occupations that summer, among them a stint as a waitress. When they all proved similarly disappointing she began to feel, as she suggests in *The Bell Jar*, that she could do nothing well except study and compile a superior academic record. When she began an earnest, unproductive study of Joyce's *Ulysses* for her honors thesis at Smith, the last shred of self-confidence withered. "I was a nothing," she explained. "A zero."

After several unsuccessful attempts to find a sure and easy death she had taken a bottle of sleeping pills to a deeply secluded spot in the basement of her mother's home in Wellesley Hills (she referred to it as a fruit cellar) and consumed them, having first left a note suggesting that she had run away. Although her family initiated a nationwide search as soon as they discovered her missing, several days passed before her brother, coming to the basement on a routine errand, heard her moans and discovered her half-dead body. "I couldn't even succeed at killing myself," she lamented. "I took too many pills and became violently ill, but didn't die, after all." In what must have been several semiconscious intervals she had struggled to rise, falling in the process and scraping her face on the concrete walls, causing the massive, gangrenous facial lacerations that left a deep brown scar jutting across one cheekbone. She did not blame others for her depression, although she admitted feeling alienated. She talked freely about her father's death when she was nine and her reactions to it. "He was an autocrat," she recalled. "I adored and despised him, and I probably wished many times that he were dead. When he obliged me and died, I imagined that I had killed him." And then she added, "The strangest part of the suicide attempt was regaining consciousness in the hospital. I don't believe in God or in an afterlife, and my first reaction when I opened my eyes was 'No, it can't be. There can't be anything after death.' I was terribly disappointed that even death couldn't put an end to my consciousness." Although she never identified the particular insights that had emerged as a result of her psychiatric treatment or discussed her relationship with her psychiatrist, she did recount an incident that in retrospect is poignant. "It seems foolish now," she said, "but I stormed into the psychiatrist's office and demanded a lobotomy—there seemed little reason to go on suffering and little hope that I would ever recover. The psychiatrist laughed at me and shook his head. 'You're not going to get off that easily,' he said." From her remarks it was clear that Sylvia herself felt that her depression had resulted

21

from an inability to maintain a sense of her own worth, particularly in the face of the high praise others invariably heaped upon her.

My own understanding of these confidences was probably an oversimplification: the remarkable intelligence and the enormous talent combined somehow to create a distorted perspective, causing Sylvia to set goals for herself that were impossibly high, perhaps deliberately so. During the previous summer she had been forced or cajoled into an untenable position, unable to react positively to the dream-come-true details of the journalism interlude but similarly unable to allow herself the luxury of failure. Too many successes, too many prizes and too many accolades going too far back had created a pattern of response that she could not break without help, as though, after all the intrigue and sorcery and effort that were necessary to find him, Cinderella discovered that she didn't want to marry the Prince, but was helpless to stop the ceremonies.

But all that was behind her in the spring of 1954. She was functioning again in top form. She was writing again and she was opening up, sharing her fears and flourishing in the safe, protected, regulated environment of dormitory life. Aside from introspection, our conversations were usually banal. We never probed any significant social or cultural problem. In spite of the almost universal implications of the McCarthy era with its pogroms and suspicions, we never exchanged political observations. Like shopgirls we worked long hours, and the diversions we sought when we relaxed were pedestrian. We pursued boys, clothes, and entertainment as energetically as we pursued an education. We were engrossed with ourselves and we noticed the world beyond our doors only when it affected or touched us. Our egoism was colossal.

When the semester ended, Sylvia invited me to spend a weekend with her at her mother's home in Wellesley Hills. We were planning to go to Harvard summer school in July, and the brief holiday offered a pleasant hiatus. Several highlights of the visit are particularly memorable. The first was a visit with Olive Higgins Prouty, the author of *Stella Dallas*. Mrs. Prouty had financed Syl's scholarship at Smith and she had also met many of the medical expenses after the suicide attempt. Syl was grateful to and indulgently fond of her famous patron, as well as obviously impressed by the financial success of *Stella Dallas*.

The afternoon at Mrs. Prouty's was typical of many afternoons Sylvia and I spent together because it illustrated a paradox in our natures. On the one hand we were scholarship students at Smith, serious scholars in whom strangers had both confidence and a financial investment. We were, presumably, the brightest and best that our generation could produce, and while we did not necessarily believe it, we were properly imperious. But underneath we were schoolgirls, come only recently from play. We were giddy and irrepressible. At times it was a huge effort to be serious and we did not always succeed in bringing it off. On this particular sunny afternoon with Mrs. Prouty, a pompous, obsequious butler served tea and canapés. Sitting there in her cavernous living room in our white gloves and our very best company manners, under the reproving gaze of the butler, we consumed a platter of tiny, delectable cucumber sandwiches in less than half an hour. Mrs. Prouty may or may not have been amused by our intemperance; at any rate, she instructed the astonished butler to bring another tray of sandwiches, which we obligingly devoured. Neither of us was being deliberately vulgar or gluttonous; the sandwiches were tasty and we simply didn't consider resisting them. We talked importantly with Mrs. Prouty about her literary career, about Smith, and about ourselves in the best approximation of small talk we could manage, punctuating our remarks with the incessant, audible crackle of crisp, paper-thin, sour-creamy cucumbers. We ate until we were half sick with cucumbers and suppressed glee. Neither of us had ever before tasted a cucumber sandwich. We were young, self-conscious, and chronically hungry. Not until after we left did the incongruity of our actions strike us as embarrassing.

The next day was my twenty-first birthday, and Sylvia wakened me with a breakfast tray and a gift package. The gift was a book: a small copy of *Alice in Wonderland*. It was inscribed, with typical Plath precision: "A classic, read-aloud heirloom to be taken in small, mirthful doses at bedtime."

Later that day we drove to Cape Cod for my first encounter with sea, sand, and salt air. Sylvia enjoyed playing the Eastern sophisticate to my Midwestern ingenue. Her earliest childhood years had been spent in a small Massachusetts seaside town and the legacy they left was an enduring familiarity with ocean creatures and their habitats. She slipped comfortably into the role of mentor, amazed at my ignorance of the mussels and clams that had been her earliest playthings. Later that summer, in Boston, I was to see the same reaction: Sylvia playing the gracious hostess, only slightly supercilious as she arranged before me a potpourri of appealing diversions.

Parks, museums, and crusty old churches came alive at her suggestion. She possessed an innate sense of history that could transform dusty, deteriorating, half-forgotten monuments into objects of wonder in the same way that she now transformed a shard of clamshell or a starfish into a miracle of craftsmanship and design. She had the poet's eye for the minutiae of nature and an ear tuned to the lyric cadences of their names: limpet, rockweed, anemone. For me, a city girl brought up in the world of asphalt and abstract ideas, it was a whole new world.

Her presentation of the Cape was flawless. Although I live today only fifteen miles from the Pacific, the first picture that comes to my mind when I hear the word "ocean" is that deserted, sandy stretch of Nauset beach, adorned only by the heavy contours of the dunes and the fringe of tangled kelp that marked its borders. We did not get to Provincetown, but Sylvia created it for me, there on the beach at Nauset. So precisely did she describe the colors, the hubbub, and the throbbing, deep-summer tenor of the place that when I did visit there, almost a year later, it was with a keen sense of *déjà vu.*

For the evening of my birthday Sylvia had arranged a double date that would reveal the pleasures of Boston at night. My escort was a young man who had been Syl's friend for a long while, possibly since childhood. She treated him in a tolerant and patronizing manner, even though he was brilliant, urbane, and irresistibly handsome. She had not selected him in an effort to play matchmaker but because his qualifications as an escort were flawless. He had accumulated a string of graduate degrees, spoke seven languages fluently, and had lived all over the world. Syl boasted of his accomplishments with almost maternal pride, and she introduced us with obvious satisfaction, as though saying, "These friends are my treasures and I want to share them." She presented me to him like a prized porcelain, with the comment, "Here she is; doesn't she have marvellously mobile plotisma?" My date laughed as if in response to a private joke, but I had to ask the meaning of "plotisma." Although I have never been able to verify the definition she offered, the compliment was memorable.

The night's activities introduced me to a variety of delights, ranging from Armenian cuisine, complete with baklava, to Turkish belly dancers and Vaughn Monroe's The Meadows. Boston was Sylvia's bailiwick and on my birthday she gave it to me, piece by fascinating piece. I was Alice, Boston was Wonderland, and Sylvia had prescribed it for me in "small, mirthful doses."

Toward the middle of July we met again in Cambridge. Syl had encouraged me to accompany her to Harvard; her plans had been made for several months when she suggested that I go, too. Hans Kohn, who had taught at Smith before my time, was offering two interesting courses at Harvard that summer, and I was eager to study under this renowned professor. I applied for and received a scholarship to match Sylvia's. Both Mrs. Plath and our housemother expressed pleasure at the news that I would be with Syl that summer. Both were concerned that the anniversary of the suicide attempt, which would fall during our stay in Cambridge, might prove a difficult hurdle for her to overcome. Both implied that I would exert a stabilizing influence on Sylvia, although I scoffed at the implication that I was going along as a sort of proctor. I was convinced that she was as normal and predictable as I.

On the surface the period was a refreshingly domestic interlude for both of us. With two other Lawrence House girls, who had summer jobs in Boston, we sublet a spacious apartment on Massachusetts Avenue in Cambridge, a five-minute walk from Harvard Square. The apartment had only one bedroom, which Syl and I appropriated, explaining that we needed a private place to study. The other girls were relegated to the dining room, where a dingy sofa could be converted into a double bed. Because Syl and I had classes only in the morning and were free in the afternoons, we volunteered to do all the cooking for the quartet. Syl had either bought or brought along a copy of *Joy of Cooking*, and when I protested that I couldn't even boil water, she assured me that anyone who could read could also cook. Each of us contributed one dollar per day to the food kitty and Syl and I split the week and the money. The arrangement was relatively successful; Syl, particularly, seemed descended from a long line of dieticians. She attacked cooking with the same zealous attention to detail that had assured the succession of poetry prizes and the Phi Beta Kappa key—as though she actually believed that anything worth doing was worth doing well.

The apartment bore the indisputable stamp of the Harvard graduate students from whom we had rented it. It was comfortably furnished in the genial, eclectic fashion of early bachelorhood, and it was clean in the obvious places. But we were passionate converts to domesticity. Eventually we found the grimy corners and dusty shelves where we could practice housekeeping. I particularly remember the kitchen floor, where alternating layers of dirt and wax had fused into a muddy abomination the color of sewage. In the first surge of domestic ardor I attacked that floor with an array of varied implements. I scraped and gouged and dug, day after day, until, in a final furious attempt, I tied steel wool pads to the bottoms of my loafers and skated my way through the waxy accumulation.

The refrigerator presented another kind of challenge. Its meager freezing compartment had shrunk noticeably through years of frost and neglect until, when we inherited it, it could barely accommodate one ice cube tray. Since it was summer and the apartment was not air-conditioned, we consumed gallons of iced drinks. To lay in an adequate supply of ice cubes each day was a severe test of our ingenuity. Defrosting the freezer was out of the question, since to do so we would have to disconnect the refrigerator, perhaps for days, losing our only flimsy protection against botulism and ptomaine. We never did solve the problem completely, but neither Syl nor I ever passed the refrigerator without taking a stab at its icy interior with whatever sharp instrument was handy.

The food was varied and nourishing; there were no complaints about our gastronomic accomplishments except once, when an eggplant and clam casserole that I prepared lay untouched on everyone's plate—a lumpy, grayish-green cud that we could not bring ourselves to taste. Syl's meals were particularly appetizing; however, as the weeks passed I realized that her culinary triumphs were imposing a handicap on my half of the week. In the effort to produce gourmet meals she was inclined to the generous use of luxury items like anchovy paste and capers. Eventually I realized she was not buying any staples during her half of the week. For a while she was obsessed with walnut halves. We had them on grapefruit in the morning, on deviled eggs at lunch, and in the dinner salad. We might not have detergent or flour, but we did have a proliferation of walnuts. I always seemed to enter my half of the week with a pressing need for five dollars' worth of necessities like paper towels and soap. Consequently, I could manage only a bare minimum at meals. Since we were obviously in competition in this area I thought the competition should be waged according to some ground rules. Syl was coolly unresponsive to my suggestion that she buy some staples with her half of the money, protesting that she was staying within her fourteen-dollar limit and that I really had no legitimate complaint. Suddenly she seemed annoyingly dense.

As the weeks passed, Syl displayed a number of other habits that were surprising if not irritating. Although the details are petty, they illustrate her preoccupation with possessions and the lengths to which she would go to keep her property and perhaps herself separate and inviolate. I bought a fifteen-cent bottle of dime-store nail polish. Admiring the color, Syl went to the store and purchased an identical bottle. When she returned home with her purchase, I was astonished to see her laboriously labeling her bottle with her name, in heavy black marking pen. The bottles were indistinguishable and we kept them on separate sides of the bedroom although I could not understand why it would be critical if one of us inadvertently used the other's polish. A similar incident occurred later in the summer when Sylvia decided to give a party to entertain some of the interesting people we had met at Harvard. She graciously included several of my friends and stipulated that she would provide and prepare all the food if I would get the apartment ready. The arrangement seemed fair: I cleaned while she created in the kitchen, and the subsequent party was a dazzling if quiet success. When it was over, Sylvia meticulously wrote her name on every leftover box of crackers and bag of potato chips, placing them high up in an obscure corner of the kitchen cupboard. As her guests, we could have eaten them at the party, but once it was over they were hers exclusively. The exclusiveness was becoming a familiar symptom. A day or two before the party I met Syl in Harvard Yard after classes and found her savagely angry.

"Did you see her?" she demanded as I walked up. "Did you see that impertinent girl who just walked off?"

I admitted that I had not noticed a particular girl.

"That awful, audacious girl," she continued, "just came up to me and said, 'I see you've got my hairdo.' Imagine that! She thinks I've got her hairdo!"

As the story came rushing out, I learned that a girl who was a complete stranger had remarked to Syl in a friendly way that Syl's rather novel hairstyle was just like her own. The remark had left her visibly shaken, and I could not understand why, except that Syl objected to having her hairstyle described as the copy.

Once, when she was in the bedroom putting away laundry, I remarked about the neat, almost mechanical arrangement of the contents of her drawers. "Yes," she confessed, "if anyone ever disarranged my things I'd feel as though I had been raped intellectually." The reaction was extreme, and it frightened me.

Our diversions in Boston were prosaic. We bought clothes in Filene's basement, ate in every inexpensive, appealing, out-of-the-way place we could find, and explored the innumerable cobwebby Cambridge nooks and crannies that offered used books and other antique treasures. As usual we played follow the leader, with Sylvia exposing me for the first time to the intricacies of life in a university town. I was quick to express delight at my discoveries and Sylvia basked in it. We rode the Park Street subway, getting off at a different stop each day to explore and exclaim. We attended Esplanade concerts, watched sailboat races on the Charles, and giggled at the profusion of signs advertising the Mystic River Bridge. Neither of us spent much time studying and Syl did little writing that summer. We were engaged in a whirlwind love affair with life that left us little time for work. We adopted a stray cat whom Syl christened Nijinsky because he leaped and pirouetted at the sight of us. We came home from class on lazy, rainy afternoons and drank hot toddies, sharing each other's thoughts. We were content to be young, to be ourselves, and to be together. For a short time that summer Cambridge was a glorious adventure and we were Siamese twins, joined at the ego.

Men figured in our lives in a motley procession. Although they were important to the life style we had adopted, I never heard Syl express strong feelings about any of the boys she dated. Her romances often seemed mere dalliances; she enjoyed male company and blossomed in its presence, but she did not appear to care deeply about any of the men she had met up to that point. She was attracted to older men; her male professors aroused about as much emotion and passionate concern as I ever heard her express. If I had been asked to select the one man in the world whom Syl most admired I would probably have chosen Richard Wilbur, the poet. She had once interviewed him for a magazine article and she talked of him often. She read every word he wrote and showed me every article about him and every photograph of him that appeared anywhere in print. At the time I imagined that Syl would someday marry a writer, although she herself seemed to think that she would eventually marry Jeffrey McGuire, a boy from Wellesley Hills whom she saw often that summer. He was intelligent, articulate, spectacularly handsome, and obviously devoted to Syl. He seemed the proper middle-class choice. Moreover, he had the one qualification that Syl considered crucial: he was well over six feet tall.

Sylvia never exhibited any of the standard hang-ups about her own height—she never stooped or sagged or wore flat-heeled shoes to appear shorter. In fact, she seemed to feel that size was an index of superiority. She had decided that her husband would be a very tall man and she spoke, half-jokingly, of producing a race of superchildren, as superlatively large as they were intelligent. The children, she predicted, would all be boys.

She saw another young man regularly while I knew her, a dark, brooding, passionate Gallic type whose brilliance and imagination were the equal of her own. She endowed him with the qualities of a Byronic hero: an air of mystery and an almost sinister melancholia that she found fascinating, even though she seemed also to regard him, at times, as an amusing toy. Because he was small and slightly built she admitted to a feeling of physical revulsion in his presence. "When he holds me in his arms," she confided, "I feel like Mother Earth with a small brown bug crawling on me." The fact that she could make such a statement suggests a link between her creativity and her behavior. Most girls would not have sustained a relationship with a young man whom they could describe with repugnance, but Sylvia was intrigued by her reaction. She could not resist exploring the bizarre or ugly, even when it frightened or sickened her, and I could not help feeling that for a girl with a delicate equilibrium it was a dangerous pastime.

Our shopgirl mentality prompted us, early in the summer, to strike a bargain—to agree that we would accept any and all dates that included an invitation to dinner or the theater, even if we found the men themselves uninteresting. We had a gluttonous appetite for the attractions of the city and little money to indulge it. We had made the pledge in a moment of high good spirits, and I did not believe that either of us was quite mercenary enough to make a habit of premeditated avarice. Still, we did not expect the men we met that summer to be important to us; Syl had practically decided to marry Jeff McGuire and I was half-engaged to a boy back home. We felt safely immune and unassailable. We flirted and charmed our way through a dozen brief encounters, enjoying the imagined stir we created as we bounced from one diversion to the next, presenting a united front to all pursuers.

The idyll was short lived. Early in August a strange, morose, determined young man entered our lives, armed with the knowledge that to divide is to conquer, exposing undercurrents in the relationship that affected it significantly.

We met him on the steps of Widener Library. After classes one morning Syl asked if I had been in the library. When I said that I had not, she propelled me inside, where she conducted a twenty-minute tour. When we emerged, a balding, myopic-looking young man was standing on the steps, wearing a woebegone expression. He was thin, with bones like broomstraws that poked out here and there along his frame. And he was tall; the splintery frame stretched up above our heads like a flagpole, ending at a small round head. His face was pinched and solemn, and in its center, behind the thickest glasses I had ever seen, two tiny, watery blue circles masqueraded as eyes. He spoke first, telling us that his name was Irwin and that he was a professor of biology at another Eastern college. He was doing research at Harvard that summer and, naturally, he was lonely. He had not spoken more than ten sentences when both Syl and I knew that he was probably the most brilliant man we had ever met. His voice was low and resonant and he used it to fashion a rhetoric that set our heads spinning. His words were a frontal assault; almost before we knew it we had accompanied him to a nearby coffee shop where we sat dumbstruck while he wooed us with his awesome understanding of subjects we hardly knew existed. Syl managed to interject a few intelligent comments, but I was tongue-tied, unable to pronounce even my name without choking on it. I felt like a mental pygmy; I couldn't understand his vocabulary, far less the elaborate theories he was explaining. Besides, something about him made me uncomfortable. For all his affable good nature there was something sinister about him that I couldn't define. Something rankled in the back of my head that I couldn't reach, going beyond the fact that he made me feel illiterate and unsure of myself. Dimly, on the very edges of consciousness, I wondered, if Irwin was as great a genius as he seemed, why he was wasting his time with us.

Despite my minor misgivings, we returned to the apartment in a gay, expansive mood, wondering which of us he would call. I was almost certain it would be Syl. I hadn't done much more than listen to his monologue, while she had at least contributed an occasional bright remark. We didn't have long to wait. When the phone rang early in the afternoon, Sylvia answered it. She chatted with him for a few moments and then handed the phone to me. Irwin issued an invitation to dinner and I heard myself accepting. I wasn't eager to go out alone with this mental marvel, but I remembered the bargain Syl and I had made and was reluctant to admit my hesitation. Syl took the news of her defeat easily; she apparently knew it was a minor skirmish.

My uneasiness increased when Irwin appeared to pick me up. He ushered me out the door and into an ancient black convertible that looked like a relic of some gangland vendetta. A small, bullet-shaped hole marred the right front windshield and bits of fluffy white upholstery popped through the seat, which looked as though someone had slashed it in a methodical search for contraband. My confidence hit rock bottom when Irwin admitted that the "dinner" to which he was taking me was to be cooked by him and served in his apartment. I cringed and shrank as far away as I could on the lumpy up-holstery. All my fragile savoir-faire disappeared. I tried to make my voice sound calm and matter-of-fact. "Irwin," I admitted, "I've never been in a man's apartment before —I mean, not a man I didn't know very well. I don't think I want to go on."

Although Irwin tried to smile encouragingly, his look suggested that he enjoyed devouring bright earnest types like me with one carnivorous gulp. "I can understand your caution," he purred, "but you'll be perfectly safe. My landlady lives right next door, and we can leave the door open if you like."

Because his response seemed genuine, I agreed to go on. When we arrived at his apartment he introduced me to his landlady, a Mrs. Orsini, who was bent over a steaming pot of spaghetti in her kitchen, just off the hall. The atmosphere was homey and comfortable, and I began to relax a little, although I wasn't about to lower my guard entirely. The dinner itself was pleasant enough, although I noticed that Irwin hovered nearby with his wine bottle poised, refilling my glass each time I swallowed. Without commenting, I began to sip more slowly. When we finished eating, Irwin seemed suddenly at a loss for words. He disposed quickly and impatiently with every subject I introduced, and I filled the awkward silences with every conversational trick I could devise. I began to worry again. Sometime in the course of the evening Irwin had closed the door without attracting my attention. Suddenly, with all the subtlety of a predatory animal, he was moving toward me, grinning terribly, and I knew I was out of my depth. A brown leather couch sat in the middle of the room, facing the fireplace. For five frightening minutes Irwin literally chased me around and around it, grabbing at me convulsively and insisting, "I always make the ladies happy." Somehow, through luck or sheer verbal tenacity, I managed to convince him that the only way he could make me happy was to take me home. Although he was pleasant and courteous during the five-minute drive, I didn't feel completely safe until I collapsed inside the door of our apartment, sobbing my fear and rage. Sylvia was solicitous and sympathetic, and the next day when Irwin called and asked for me she delivered the message that I would not talk to him.

As the days passed, he continued to call, and I noticed that Sylvia's conversations with him were growing longer. She began seeing him furtively, as though embarrassed by her defection. Once, after a particularly intimate telephone conversation with him she turned to me and said, as if to dispel my doubts, "I don't know why you couldn't manage a platonic relationship with Irwin. I'm having no trouble." She was seeing her psychiatrist regularly that summer, and I once asked if she had told the doctor about Irwin. "Of course," she insisted. "Who do you think drives me to my appointments?"

My uneasiness persisted in spite of her reassurances. I was certain that if she had been fond of Irwin, or even liked him, she would have waged a campaign to win me over. The fact that she never talked about him suggested that she found nothing to defend. Although he had frightened me badly, I was willing to accept the possibility that my experience with him was not typical or that Sylvia brought out his nobler instincts. I was not normally shocked when the boys I dated appeared to have sexual appetites, but Irwin was different. His approach was calculating and impersonal, like a depraved hobby he pursued night after night—a succession of nameless, faceless conquests carved into the bedpost. I believed that I had narrowly escaped being raped and I was afraid that Sylvia was in danger. I did not voice my fears because the rules of schoolgirl friendship forbid meddling. Although I thought Sylvia was out of her depth with Irwin as much as I had been, I also understood that she was stubborn and competitive enough to enjoy succeeding where I had failed. If the domestication of Irwin gave her pleasure, my warnings would have been ignored or, worse, attributed to jealousy. But my anxiety did not subside. If anything, the crisis seemed to be accelerating. When she acquired a key to his apartment, explaining that she needed a private place to study, I could almost feel the tensions building.

One morning I wakened to find that Syl's bed had not been slept in. I guessed her whereabouts, although such a blatant indiscretion was unlike her. When the phone rang several moments later, I was only mildly surprised to hear Irwin's voice.

"Nancy," he said, his voice dripping unction, "Sylvia wanted you to know that she got sick in my apartment last night and had to see a doctor. He felt she should stay here all night, but she's all right now, and she'll be home soon."

Although he seemed reluctant to say more, I insisted. "What happened?" I asked impatiently. "What was wrong with her?"

Either Irwin thought quickly or the response had been rehearsed. "She started to hemorrhage," he explained.

"But she's fine now." Before I could press for more details, he hung up.

When I came home from class about eleven, I found a note from Syl saying that she was better and that she and Irwin had gone to the beach for a picnic. I tried not to worry and spent the afternoon attempting to study. When she came in about five she looked dreadful. Her color had faded; a chalky pallor lay over her normally tanned skin like a dusting of talcum and her dark eyes had burrowed even deeper into their sockets, like two frightened ferrets. When I asked how she felt she admitted that the bleeding had become heavy again. I walked with her to the bedroom, where she sat down wearily on the bed. For a few minutes we chatted innocuously and I asked no questions. When she got up, a large dark stain had spread across the place where she had been sitting. The back of her skirt was bloodstained and a small trickle of blood ran down her leg like the outline of a jagged tear. Still she seemed irritated rather than alarmed. She washed and changed into a nightgown and robe and we went out to join our roommates in the dining room for dinner. Although she tried to appear charmingly normal at the table, I could see her growing weaker. Suddenly she got up and hurried to the bathroom. A moment later we heard a crash that sent me racing after her.

I found her on the bathroom floor in a pool of blood that spread like a giant wound across the regular, hexagonal white tiles of the bathroom floor and walls. She made no attempt to get up, but lay there, a crimson apparition, her fear filling the small room like a third person.

When she spoke her voice was very small, as though each word had been framed in a faraway place. "Nancy," she said, "I think I'm bleeding to death. You have to help me."

"Of course I'll help you," I assured her. "But I have to know what's wrong. What's causing the bleeding?"

She didn't hesitate. "He raped me," she explained.

I didn't comment as she went on. "We went to see a gynecologist last night when the bleeding started and he thought he had it stopped. But now it's worse than ever!"

"Well, let's not sit here talking about it," I suggested. "Tell me who the doctor was and I'll call and ask him what we do now."

At my words, Sylvia became hysterical. All the stored-up fear and vulnerability came pouring out in a confusing helter-skelter of words and sobs. At first she was incoherent; then the bits and pieces of her terror took on names and shapes: doctors, hospitals, medical instruments. It was as if all the commonplace machinery of the profession that had diagnosed and treated her wretchedness of the summer before had somehow absorbed her misery, as if her emotional problems had not been solved but had merely been lifted from her, and hidden away in some antiseptic storage room, to be clamped down upon her again in an unsuspecting moment. Her horror of doctors and hospitals was so profound that it almost seemed she would rather bleed to death than encounter them again. With my heart pounding I tried to convince her that she was in more danger from the blood than from the fear and that I would call another doctor if she could not tell me the name of the one she had seen the night before. Finally she grew quiet, speaking the doctor's name in a voice that was flat and empty. I looked up his number and was about to dial it when she called me back into the bathroom.

"There's one more thing you should know," she admitted. "After last summer I can't stand any more publicity or notoriety, so I gave the doctor a fictitious name."

"That doesn't matter," I assured her. "Just tell me what name you used and I'll use it, too."

"That's just the trouble," she sobbed. "I can't remember."

Caught up in the tangled web she had woven, I went back to the phone and called the doctor. When he answered I explained Syl's predicament, without mentioning her name, saying only that she had needed to conceal her identity and could not remember what name she had used. He was sympathetic and understanding, and he told me in graphic terms what to do to stop the bleeding.

I went back to Sylvia, helped her change into a yellow nylon nightgown, and did what the doctor had told me to do. The task was neither pleasant nor easy. I had never seen so much blood, and I certainly wasn't skilled in the techniques of the midwife. Sylvia was compliant and relaxed, although I had to force myself to remain calm and appear efficient, afraid that any sign of weakness or uncertainty on my part would unleash another torrent of emotion from her. I quite literally felt the pulsating current that ran between us as I supported and sustained her. From seven until ten Sylvia lay on the bed, which we had covered with an old plastic tablecloth. She chatted amiably, without a trace of the fear that had surfaced earlier, while I sat beside her, occasionally check-

41

ing for the ominous signs that the bleeding had resumed. We talked of many things, but each time I mentioned Irwin she changed the subject. At ten she decided to get up. She stood, wobbling at first and then careening against the wall as we both noticed that she had been lying in her own blood. Unable to soak into the plastic tablecloth, the blood had seeped under her, forming a large incriminating pool; when she rose it flowed and eddied along the contours the weight of her body had pressed into the bed. The back of her yellow nightgown dripped bright red and bits of dried blood were matted in her long yellow hair. I knew that she had lost a dangerous amount of blood and I was afraid that she would bleed to death unless we got help very quickly. I raced to the phone and called the doctor again, praying that he would be in. He was, and he agreed to meet us at the hospital in ten minutes. Back in the bedroom, when I told Syl we were going to the hospital, she was shaken by another wave of terror, which she managed to control only when I promised to stay with her every single minute. Then she remembered a detail I had overlooked.

"How are we going to get there?" she asked feebly.

I had not thought about transportation. Sylvia couldn't walk, we had no car, and a taxi might be too long coming. I could think of only one person whom we could ask to drive us. "Irwin will have to take us," I said. Then I was on the phone again, commanding Irwin to get to our apartment as soon as possible, explaining that Sylvia had to get to the hospital immediately.

He was there in less than five minutes. He helped me get Sylvia into a coat and out to the car, where he lifted her into the front seat. I climbed into the back, and none of us spoke on the way to the hospital. When we got there, Irwin stayed in the car and an orderly helped Syl into a wheelchair. We had to stop at the registration desk to give Syl's name and address before she could be wheeled into the emergency room. We gave another fictitious name and our Cambridge address. When the nurse behind the desk asked to whom the bill should be sent, I didn't hesitate. "To Irwin," I snapped. Weakly, Syl gave the nurse his name and address.

Although she seemed calmer now, she still refused to go to the emergency room unless I accompanied her. I didn't want to waste time arguing and the hospital staff did not object. The orderly wheeled Sylvia to a room around the corner and placed her on an examining table as a doctor emerged from the shadows, introducing himself to me and greeting Syl as though she were a patient of long standing. I stood at the top of the table, beside Syl's head, holding her hand as he administered the emergency treatment, which he assured us would stop the bleeding once and for all. The procedure took about ten minutes, during which the doctor kept up an easy banter, encouraging us to relax. The metal instruments clanked in his hand like a fistful of silverware, but he seemed to know what he was doing. The job completed, he flashed us a conspiratorial smile.

"Tomorrow you'll be good as new," he remarked. "And don't start thinking you're exceptional. I've seen a number of cases just like yours."

Although the remark was intended to reassure, it seemed to me the final irony in an evening full of them.

I walked out to the waiting room while Syl exchanged a few more pleasantries with the doctor. Then I helped her out to Irwin's car and we drove silently home. At the door of our apartment Irwin turned to me.

"I'll call tomorrow to see how she is," he promised. I had to force myself to spit out an answer.

"Don't bother," I said vehemently, "you've done enough."

Inside, our roommates were waiting. All the bloody evidence of the episode had been removed; even the bathroom had regained its scrupulous white monotony. I was enormously grateful that we hadn't come back to face any physical reminders of the ordeal and I wondered which of the girls had done the work. I felt suddenly guilty that they had been left with the grubby, menial aftermath of the episode when they could not be trusted to know its details. All through the evening Syl had motioned them away, unable or unwilling to allow them even to guess what was happening. In a way, it had been like that all summer. Although the four of us got along remarkably well together in a superficial way, it was obvious that Syl and I had formed an association from which they were excluded. Syl was cordial and pleasant to them, but she was also distant, pulling away at the slightest suggestion of familiarity. I hadn't done much better. My friendships, too, tended to be either profound or nonexistent, and at the moment Syl was all I could manage.

The two of them were a study in contrasts as they sat there on the couch waiting for us to explain the evening's events. Sue, who was three years younger than we, was a bulky, hearty, physically energetic girl who roared across the surface of life, enjoying it tremendously and taking people at face value. But Mary Ann, another senior from Lawrence House, was a different story. She was timid and soft-spoken, a girl whose protective environment had shielded her from unpleasantness until very recently. She was bright, intuitive, and fragile, and I could read the fascination and distaste mingled in her appraising glance as we walked into the room. She had had a difficult time assimilating even the intellectual shocks of academic life at Smith, and I sensed that our dinner-table conversations that summer had seemed to her a bewildering succession of iconoclasms and irreverences. She seemed to be in a constant state of agitation in Syl's presence, groping for easy answers that would not come, unable to locate in her catalog of absolutes a clue to Syl's ambivalence. Trained to regard life in terms of either/or, Mary Ann was both fascinated and disturbed by the apparently endless variety of Syl's attitudes and the nagging complexity of her ideas, yet she was unable to shut out their disquieting implications. I could understand why. Sylvia's personality was powerful and difficult to ignore. Her remarks conveyed a sense of urgency and her smallest concerns inevitably became emergencies to anyone who shared them. The poetic eye was always at work examining nuance and measuring obscure detail, turning observation into ultimatum. Sue was blithely unaffected, but Mary Ann caught every notion Syl threw out, however painful or hard to reconcile with the set of values that had reduced all her previous experience to a choice of simple alternatives, automatic and unequivocal.

If she had braced herself on this particular evening to struggle with the details of Syl's misfortune, Mary Ann was to be disappointed. We concocted an explanation full of evasion and half-truths that seemed to satisfy both girls. Then we went into the bedroom, closing the door behind us. Before we fell asleep, Syl told me that she had to go back to the hospital at noon the next day to have the packing removed and that she expected me to go with her.

"But I can't, Syl," I explained. "Tomorrow at noon I'm having lunch with Hans Kohn. Have you forgotten?"

I'd told Professor Kohn that I would be doing my honors thesis the next year on Morris Cohen, a Jewish philosopher-educator who was a personal friend of his. Professor Kohn had offered to share his reminiscences over lunch. The information could be very important to my research and I had looked forward to the meeting for weeks, flattered to be receiving special attention from my famous teacher.

As she listened to my words, Syl paled and began to cry. The fear rushed out once more in a torrent of staccato sentences.

"I can't go there alone," she wailed. "I just can't. You don't understand how I feel about hospitals. If you were really my friend you wouldn't desert me when I need you."

Eventually she agreed to a compromise. I persuaded her that we could go to the hospital at ten and be back in time for my luncheon appointment. As we walked to the hospital the next morning Syl was her usual ebullient self. The medical procedure took only a moment and the ordeal was ended. I assumed we would never see Irwin again.

If the incident caused Sylvia any emotional trauma she

recovered from it quickly. I wasn't quite so fortunate; I kept seeing her blood on the regular white tiles of the bathroom and hearing her anguished voice as she pleaded with me to keep her from dying. More than anything else, I was troubled by the suspicion that Syl had not learned anything from the episode. She was seeing Irwin again before the week was over and also boasting that she had become innocently involved with a Harvard professor whose wife, jumping to an erroneous conclusion, called her "the blond bitch." Syl found the epithet, as well as the circumstances, curiously amusing, while I sank deeper into a state of perpetual alarm, girding myself for the next crisis.

I did not believe that Syl was as adventurous as she seemed; the middle-class conventions were too deeply ingrained in her nature to be easily shed. She enjoyed stalking danger and was not as adept at last-minute escapes as she imagined. She must have felt particularly secure that summer, as though my presence provided a safety that might otherwise have been missing. As long as I was there to put the pieces back together and shove the fear back down into the crevices where she kept it, she could experiment, or pretend to, without worrying about the consequences. She wanted desperately to live up to the expectations of a society that viewed her as a bright, charming, enormously talented disciple of bourgeois conformity. On the other hand, she ached to experience life in all its grim and beautiful complexity. The conflict was painful and unremitting. If she seemed to be resolving the conflict that summer, in a burst of new-found confidence, the effect was illusory. Her confidence might be increasing, but mine was disappearing. I was drained and exhausted and it was an exhaustion that sleep would not cure.

One evening, I was alone in the apartment when the telephone rang. It was Mrs. Plath, asking to speak to Syl. When I said she wasn't there and I didn't know where she was, Mrs. Plath was incredulous, reminding me that it was the anniversary of the suicide attempt and that someone ought to be keeping an eye on Syl. As the conversation continued, Mrs. Plath's incredulity turned to anxiety. She persuaded me to try to locate Syl immediately, and she also asked if I thought Syl was "all right" emotionally. When I said that I did, she asked if I could absolutely guarantee that Syl was not off in a secluded corner of Boston that very minute, dying from some self-inflicted wound. I couldn't offer such a guarantee, and I became alarmed, too. During the next fifteen minutes I made at least twenty frantic calls to everyone Syl knew in Boston, urging her friends, in turn, to call everyone they knew who might be able to furnish a clue to her whereabouts. I knew only that she was out with Jeff McGuire and that they were stopping at a number of parties on their way to his parents' home in Wellesley Hills for dinner. I began to feel as though I was standing in front of a giant switchboard with all its circuits plugged into my vital centers. Mrs. Plath called back several times to see if I had had any success, and finally I reached Sylvia, who called her mother and offered the assurances I hadn't been able to give. The irony of the situation struck me forcibly, although Mrs. Plath's concern was understandable. Reaching out for a concrete enemy she had fastened on a particular date in August, directing her anger and concern toward the circumstances of her daughter's suffering because its causes were a nebulous, imprecise mass of attitudes that Sylvia herself could not identify.

Nevertheless, Mrs. Plath's questions had set me wondering. A chill settled along my bones as I allowed myself to imagine the consequences if I were wrong—if Syl were approaching another breakdown that I had failed to anticipate. What she was doing and feeling seemed far different from the events and attitudes of the previous summer as she described them to me. She was not depressed or alienated; in fact, she was racing from experience to experience with a recklessness that asserted her invincibility. If her almost pathological dependence was draining me, that was a different matter. I interpreted the eccentricities in her behavior as personality problems or remnants of immaturity or human imperfections, not as symptoms of emotional illness. I also viewed her relationship with her psychiatrist as a certain remedy for any problem and I assumed that she told the doctor everything she experienced and everything she thought.

Later that month, on the morning of my final exams, I was wakened by screams coming from the dining room. I rushed out to find Sue and Mary Ann standing by in stunned silence as Syl lay contorted on the bed, her cries a mixture of recrimination and pain.

"My head is flying off," she shrieked. "I can't stand the pain. Do something; I'm dying."

I ran to the phone in genuine alarm, convinced that Syl needed a doctor who could identify the cause of her pain and give her something to cure it. The first doctor I tried announced that if Syl was too ill to get to his office she should be taken to the hospital, in an ambulance if necessary. I knew better than to make that suggestion, so I kept trying. Eventually I found a doctor who promised to make a house call in an hour or so. Syl insisted that I stay with her until he arrived, ignoring my objection that my first exam began at eight. She had little tolerance for physical pain; using all her energies merely to exist, she had no reserves from which to draw in an emergency. Even minor pain seemed the final, intolerable straw that could topple her flimsy defenses. The pain generated fear, exposing a hidden level of reality where she was most vulnerable. On this particular morning, stretched there on the bed with her head throbbing, Sylvia's reasoning was simple: I could not possibly leave to take an exam when she needed me there, allied with her against the fear and pain.

The decision to leave her was probably the hardest I have ever had to make. I knew I had done everything I could and I was certain, even if she was not, that she could handle the situation without me. Mary Ann agreed to stay with her until the doctor came, and even though Syl did not agree to the arrangement, I walked out. I hurried off to my exam, alarmed not so much by Syl's headache as by the fact that she evidently viewed my leaving as a desertion. She had tested my affection and in her eyes I had failed, even though I did not be- lieve that she would attempt suicide while I was gone or die of a headache. When I returned to the apart- ment after my exam she had gone off to class. The doctor had come, given her some pills, and dispelled the pain. As far as she was concerned, the incident was forgotten.

I could not forget it so easily. Each time I put together

the puzzling pieces of Syl's behavior I constructed a picture in which she was driven, periodically, to stage a symbolic salvation with herself as the suffering victim and me as the deliverer, almost as though only by being snatched from the brink of death could she confirm her worth. Perhaps the fact that these trials always competed with some major event in my life was coincidental, but I found myself wondering if I could support Sylvia's ego and my own as well. Crisis had followed crisis that summer in a dizzying profusion, and each one left me with energies diminished. Because they provided creative inspiration, Syl plunged into situations that she could not handle emotionally. She emerged from them wounded and shaken and screaming for help. I could not escape the feeling that she was asking me to play God. She seemed to be saying that, inside the mass of complex, highly developed machinery that was Sylvia Plath a piece was missing—the key that could wind it all up and keep it going. I don't know whether I was saddened or relieved by the realization that I couldn't provide that key, but I knew I could not promise to do what no one could do without suffering severe emotional consequences. I could not promise to keep her going like some intricate, erratic timepiece and I could not face the guilt that would result if I failed to try. So I drew back instinctively, allowing some distance to come between us like an invisible barrier. Although we were roommates in Lawrence House the following year our friendship was formal and constrained. We never again lived in each other's pockets as we had throughout that Cambridge summer.

Senior year was busy and difficult for both of us. We were both writing honors theses, and Syl was working with a member of the English department on a volume of poetry that she assembled, day by day, in a blue loose-leaf notebook. I was wakened practically every morning by the sound of her typewriter. She worked furiously, slipping into her spot behind the typewriter in every spare moment. Sometimes I had to pry her away from it for meals or for sleep; the floodgates were open and she was reluctant to stop writing when the words were coming.

As far as I could tell, it was a serene year for Syl and a productive one as well. Once again, diligence brought rewards. She graduated summa cum laude and collected the usual assortment of prizes, among them a Fulbright fellowship, which she would use for a year of study at Cambridge University. I remember the day she took the examination that would determine her eligibility for the Fulbright. Examinations were not usually a worry, but this one was particularly important, and she prepared for it with a nervous flurry, trying to cram a few more facts into a mind that could already disgorge enough literary detail to fill an encyclopedia. The test itself took half a day or more; when she returned to the house at its conclusion, little wrinkles of concentration were etched around her eyes and she looked indignant. While she had obviously done well on the test as a whole, certain questions had bothered her because they concerned authors whom she did not know. One such question concerned C. P. Snow, whom she had never heard of. The wording of the test suggested that he was quite important in Great Britain, and Syl was incredulous that she could have overlooked him. Before the day ended she had re-searched him thoroughly.

One unpleasant thread ran through the year, a minor irritation that tugged sharply on the periphery of Sylvia's day-to-day experience, disturbing its equanimity. Although she was undeniably the most illustrious member of the senior class in Lawrence House, Sylvia did face some competition from Gloria Brown, or "Brownie," the leader of the beatnik fringe. Sylvia's province was one of literary competitions and high academic achievement. Although she was generally well liked and accepted by the other girls, who found her approachable if sometimes preoccupied, Sylvia did not possess the instincts of leadership. Her pursuits were solitary. Although she had a head full of exciting ideas and strong opinions, she vented them at the typewriter, rather than in an effort to attract disciples. Brownie, on the other hand, collected followers in a noisy throng. Both girls were titans, and they presented a striking contrast as they moved through Lawrence House that year. Like the clash of opposing cultures, their encounters generated a current that all of us who knew them could feel.

Brownie was the daughter of a rather well-known if temporarily penniless actor, a fact that gave her a measure of inherited fame. But she was also an extraordinary person in her own right. She was not a product of the middle class, with its carefully circumscribed manners and morals. Having grown up among the independent, unconventional inhabitants of the theatrical world, she had adopted a set of principles and ideals that were rare in our generation. Her integrity was personal and uncompromising. Brownie did not recognize any laws except those that were the product of her own nature; no bourgeois compulsion to wear shoes or to behave properly clouded her understanding of right and wrong. Having effectively removed the pretense and affectation from her own life, Brownie set to work peeling the layers of civilization from the people she encountered, using her caustic wit and a seemingly inexhaustible supply of practical jokes as her weapons. Her verbal sallies were sharp, pointed barbs that invariably hit their targets, deflating the pompous and embarrassing the self-important. To me she attached the nickname "Bungler"; sensing my eager desire to do everything well, she publicly magnified my slightest error until eventually she persuaded me to laugh at imperfection rather than deplore it. I liked her very much. Sylvia, however, saw her as a gross and irritating reminder that some people preferred revolt to a career of paralyzing conformity.

To Brownie, Sylvia was a misguided child who allowed an external force to condition her behavior, even when that force ran contrary to instinct. She seemed certain that Syl would be happier if she weren't constantly torn between her impulses and the set of values she had acquired from society. A crucial and ironic difference marked the attitudes of these two startlingly different young women. Sylvia could not guess that society would ever change; she seemed to see the taboos and tensions of her background as permanent conditions that could never be substantially altered, and she bore them with surface resignation. Brownie, on the other hand, seemed to sense the changes that were already stirring underfoot. She flitted excitedly on the first wave of a new and radical movement, like a prophet who could see ahead into the '60's and '70's, while Sylvia looked back, absorbed in the events and attitudes of the '30's and '40's, unaware of any embryonic alternative to their platitudes and pieties.

To describe what happened between these two girls as a power struggle would be misleading, since they exercised what power they had in entirely different ways. Still, the tension between them became a palpable presence in the house, an ideological tug of war that was fascinating to watch. Syl was haughtily contemptuous of Brownie. She lay in wait, like a hungry cat, hoping to catch Brownie in the violation of some house rule, an indiscretion serious enough to have major repercussions. For her part, Brownie was content to accost Syl verbally, challenging her closely held convictions, and to lead surreptitious forays into Sylvia's bedroom citadel, where, like a troupe of mischievous schoolboys chafing under the domination of a stern headmaster, she and her friends would disarrange and pillage, disturbing the neat, methodical arrangement of Syl's belongings, correctly assessing her vulnerability in this area. Although Syl never mentioned these attacks, she must have guessed who was responsible for them and waited for a chance to retaliate. For months the confrontation was a draw, until one April evening when Syl discovered Brownie and her friends drinking milk punch that they had laced with Cuban rum, smuggled into the house after a spring holiday. She threatened to report the offense, relenting only after a great deal of pressure, and after learning that Brownie, not so easily taken, had amassed a store of incriminating evidence to use against her in reprisal.

On commencement day Sylvia wakened me early in the

morning complaining of severe abdominal cramps. She asked if I had any medicine she could take that would help get her through the exercises. I said I hadn't, but suggested that some of Brownie's leftover rum might be the very thing to take. Sylvia looked at me in disbelief. "Are you crazy?" she asked. "Brownie wouldn't give me anything if I were dying—especially not any of the rum I almost reported her for having."

"You don't understand Brownie," I replied. "If you're in pain she'll give you anything she has."

She was thoughtful for a moment. "Maybe you're right," she admitted, "but I can't ask her for it. Would you ask her for me? You can tell her the rum is for you."

"No," I said gently. "I'll tell her it's for you and she'll give it to you. Wait here."

I went down the hall and explained the problem to Brownie. Without hesitating she reached under a pile of dirty clothes in the corner and pulled out the bottle, which was still half full. "Tell Syl to take what she needs," she offered. I went back to our room and told Syl what Brownie had said. I don't remember if she commented then, but she drank some of the rum and began to feel better.

A few moments later we put on our caps and gowns and descended the steps to the quadrangle for the ceremonies. We had chosen Adlai Stevenson from a long list of names to give the address, and we listened, properly dignified and attentive, as he described the lives that lay before us. If they were not exactly the lives we had visualized, at least they would make use of the educations we had received. Our unanimous vocation, as Governor Stevenson saw it, was to be wives and mothers—thoughtful, discriminating wives and mothers who would use what we had learned in government and history and sociology courses to influence our husbands and children in the direction of rationality. Men, he claimed, are under tremendous pressure to adopt the narrow view; we would help them to resist it and we would raise children who were reasonable, independent, and courageous. The speech was eloquent and impressive and we loved it even if it seemed to hurl us back to the satellite role we had escaped for four years—second-class citizens in a man's world where our only possible achievement was a vicarious one.

When commencement was over and we had returned to our room for the last time, Sylvia approached me with a question. "What am I going to do," she asked, "to let Brownie know how I misjudged her?"

"Write her a note, Syl," I suggested. "You're good at that."

A few minutes later, after Sylvia had left, Brownie came into our room carrying a small lace-trimmed handkerchief and a piece of paper. "Look, Bungler," she said in a voice full of surprise. "Look what I just found on my pillow." She handed me the handkerchief and the note, which said simply, "Thank you for teaching me humility." It was signed, "Sylvia."

I never saw her again. For several years I followed her poetic career with avid attention, seeking in her work some indication that she had found a serene and integrated center that could sustain her. For a short while in the late 1950's her work did seem less haunted—less a vehicle for her personal torment, and I was hopeful that life in England, her marriage, and her children might have strengthened her fragile grip on life. In some ways, Sylvia was the product of her times, like many of her contemporaries who chafed under a superimposed behavioral code that was both stringent and ambiguous, furtively modifying it to meet their needs and developing a code of their own that was equally rigorous. She was the appropriate spokesman for a generation of disaffected, alienated young people who kept their recalcitrant impulses inside and showed a passive, submissive face in public. In one respect, however, her attitudes were different. We believed passionately as a generation that man's humanity made him special and that he should not be dehumanized or used as a means to acquire pleasure or power. In her darker moments, Sylvia seemed to regard man as an object that could be manipulated at will. She absorbed the essence of people like doses of a unique psychedelic drug designed to expand her consciousness. Sometimes she seemed to forget that they had emotions and wills of their own.

When Sylvia died, a mutual friend from Lawrence House called to tell me, repeating what she had been told: Syl had died of pneumonia. Although the explanation did not sit too well, I accepted it rather than probe for facts that might be more painful. Not until her photograph jumped out at me from the pages of *Time* somewhat later did I learn the truth—that the torment and the talent had exacted their final toll. Throughout her life they were twin demons that nourished and provoked each other. In a sense she was the victim of an obsessive talent that sent her out into the world to gather sensations and seek wounds that could provide creative inspiration. Having acquired the wounds she stuck her fingers into them, turning the pain and blood into lines of highly subjective poetry that both repel and fascinate the reader. When the pain and blood became too intense she cried for help. I always believed that a succession of loving friends would find themselves responding to that cry as I did for a brief and painful time. I do not believe that Sylvia meant to die, and I suspect that when she did die, on that bleak and lonely February day when she stuck her head into the oven, it was because no one was there to pull her out—to submit to the final macabre threat: "I'll die if you desert me."

Afterword

Sylvia Plath would have been a good poet even if she had not committed suicide, but not exactly the poet she has since become. Our knowledge of her suicide comments on the poetry as we read it. The image of the poet that rises out of the poetry as we read it wears the aspect of her fate. Our knowledge of her suicide not only clarifies what she said and what she meant—it also certifies that she meant what she said. Or so it seemed. Additional knowledge of the poet as it comes to us has had the effect of suggesting that she meant something else, or at least something in addition. Even the suicide that seemed to clarify the poetry is no longer the one we first read about, that of a dissenting voice refuting a bad world by silencing itself, according to some, or that of a desperate woman signaling for help with a gesture that put her beyond the reach of any helping hand, according to others.

Moreover, the image of the poet that rises out of the poetry and the memory of Sylvia Plath as recorded by her friends never quite came together, even when they did seem to cast a kind of light on each other. But Nancy Hunter Steiner's *A Closer Look at Ariel* increases the area of overlap considerably; and it helps us to understand why the poet in the poetry and the poet in the memoirs of her friends often seem like two different people. It suggests a way of fitting the biography in the memoirs and the autobiography in the poems into the figure of a single life, although one that experienced itself as double. For Sylvia Plath was not only aware of an opposition between the life of her poetry and the life she led—she harnessed this opposition to charge her themes and to shape the forms of her verse.

Ted Hughes, in some remarks on the chronological order of Sylvia Plath's, his wife's, poetry notes that "the opposition of a prickly, fastidious defence and an imminent volcano is, one way or another, an element in all her early poems." The earlier the poems, as we can now see, the more powerful the defensive forces of containment. In the poems up to about 1961 or so, the defense is both formal and thematic. Those elaborate stanzas, the measured harmonics, the connoisseur's diction helped to keep the volcano from becoming more than imminent. "Throughout *The Colossus*," says A. Alvarez, "she is using her art to keep the disturbance, out of which she made her verse, at a distance." But in "Ouija," a poem written after most of those in *The Colossus*, a poem that displays the fops and gauds of Wallace Stevens' "Le Monocle de Mon Oncle" only to bring them down, we can see the distance close. We can see the defensive aureate poetry absorbed by the forces it contains, not only in what she says, but also in how she says it:

The old god, too, writes aureate poetry
In tarnished modes, maundering among the wastes,
Fair chronicler of every foul declension.
Age, and ages of prose, have uncoiled

His talking whirlwind, abated his excessive temper
When words, like locusts, drummed the darkening air
And left the cobs to rattle, bitten clean.
Skies once wearing a blue, divine hauteur
Ravel above us, mistily descend,
Thickening with motes, to a marriage with the mire.

Two poems written by Plath in March 1961, a year or
so after "Ouija," and while she was in a hospital recover-
ing from an appendectomy, were, says Ted Hughes, "the
first sign of what was on its way." She wrote these at
top speed, without her usual studies over the thesaurus,
"as one might write an urgent letter. From then on, all
her poems were written in this way." One of these two
poems, "In Plaster," alludes to the condition of a woman
in a bed near Plath's own, but takes the form of a monologue by the imminent volcano on the subject of its relations to the prickly defense—relations that have become
close, explicit, and murderous:

I shall never get out of this! There are two of me now:
This new absolutely white person and the old yellow one.

The white person, notes the lady within her cast, "is
certainly the superior one." "She is one of the real saints."
At first the old yellow one didn't like the plaster saint.
She thought her cold; "she had no personality"; she took
punishment without complaint—"you could tell almost
at once she had a slave mentality." But the yellow one
comes to realize that what her visible (and showy) saintly
self wanted was to be loved by her. She begins to take
advantage of the situation. She allows the plaster saint to
wait on her, to put "her tidiness and calmness and her
patience" at the yellow one's disposal, and the saint just

adores being so used. But in time their relationship becomes "more intense":

> She stopped fitting me so closely and seemed offish.
> I felt her criticizing me in spite of herself,
> As if my habits offended her in some way.

The trouble, as the yellow one begins to understand, was that her beautiful façade "thought she was immortal":

She wanted to leave me, she thought she was superior,
And I'd been keeping her in the dark, and she was resent-
　ful—
Wasting her days, waiting on a half-corpse!
And secretly she began to hope I'd die.

But the buried self is not in any position to dispose of her character armor—"She'd supported me for so long I was quite limp"—so she lies low, takes care not to do anything that might upset her domineering and fastidious slave, and plots her revenge. For the meantime,

Living with her was like living with my own coffin:
Yet I still depended upon her, though I did it regretfully.

Old yellow is forced to give up the idea that the two of them might make a go of it, even if they were so close, even if what they had between them was a kind of marriage—"Now I see it must be one or the other of us":

> She may be a saint, and I may be ugly and hairy,
> But she'll soon find out that that doesn't matter a bit.
> I'm collecting my strength; one day I shall manage
> 　without her,
> And she'll perish with emptiness then, and begin to
> 　miss me.

For a poem written quickly, as one might write an urgent letter, "In Plaster" is remarkable for its control, its intelligence, its grim humor and wry self-consciousness, all of which make it that much more chilling. The spiteful childishness of the anticlimactic last few words ("and begin to miss me"), an expression of the sentiment that lies behind many suicides, shows that the author, if not the speaker, realized how unlikely it was that the yellow one could dispose of the plaster saint without disposing of itself. And in *Ariel*, in which the ugly and hairy repressed self exacts its revenge against the restraints that had held it both down and together, the special horror and fascination derive from the fact that Sylvia Plath knew what was happening to her, knew where it would end, but could or would not do anything about it.

Could or would not do anything, that is, but find words for what was happening and anticipate the end. In poem after poem, from about 1959 on, one self will emerge into words and note that

I inhabit

  The wax image of myself, a doll's body.
  Sickness begins here:

Old yellow may pause on a bridge and look down out of its stiff cast toward the water, only to

      encounter one
  Blue and improbable person

  Framed in a basketwork of cattails.
  O she is gracious and austere,
  Seated beneath the toneless water!
  It is not I, it is not I.

Instead of disavowal, there may be a reluctant recognition:

This woman who meets me in windows—she is neat.

So neat she is transparent, like a spirit.
How shyly she superimposes her neat self
On the inferno of African oranges, the heel-hung pigs.
She is deferring to reality.
It is I, it is I—

Most commonly, however, a tense and lucid intelligence
will gather to a point from between and around the
opposed selves to observe how

> Daylong a duet of shade and light
> Plays between these.

or to ask "What am I to make of these contradictions?"
or eagerly to watch "My selves dissolving, old whore
petticoats," or to note, with distaste, how

> the same self unfolds like a suit
Bald and shiny, with pockets of wishes,

Notions and tickets, short circuits and folding mirrors.

Or to explain to a lover

> how you insert yourself
> Between myself and myself.

In "Two Sisters of Persephone," a poem written after
those in *The Colossus* and before those in *Ariel*, the consciousness hovering in the charged area between herself
and herself looks both ways, drawn by the positive but
held back by what Sylvia Plath took to be the negative
pole of her being. One sister of Persephone, "Bronzed as

earth," out in the bright air, couched in grasses, lulled by poppies, becomes the sun's bride, bears him a king. The other sister, a poet of sorts, sits in a dark room, works problems on "A mathematical machine," her squint eyes rat-shrewd, her meager frame root-pale, until finally, bitter, "sallow as any lemon,"

> wry virgin to the last,
> Goes graveward with flesh laid waste,
> Worm-husbanded, yet no woman.

The persona speaking out of any given poem by Sylvia Plath, then, may be either sulphurous old yellow, or the plaster saint, or a consciousness that sometimes contains these two and sometimes lies stretched between them. In the course of a given poem, especially if it is a later one, any of these personae may dissolve, re-form, take on novel shapes, fuse with whatever it is not, or reverse its charge, so that the plaster saint becomes a golden girl and squint-eyed old yellow becomes a queen bee, a comet, God's lioness. The outer shell of consciousness may be completely or dimly aware of the chthonic presence within: it may feel itself a puppet jerked by strings receding into an interior distance where a familiar demon sits in possession, or it may try to locate the menace outside of itself, among shadows, thin people, reflections in water, ghostly presences glimpsed from the corner of the mind, but always with a sense of *déjà vu*.

As they appear in the poems and prose, these opposed selves are fabulous, mythological in their dimensions and resonance; it is easy enough to sink them in traditions and arrange them among analogues. Sylvia Plath was a well-read woman. At one time she had a liking for D. H.

Lawrence, in whose work a black, father-haunted, sexy troglodyte strives to break through the encrustations of a white, supercivilized consciousness, which he associated with his mother. Before her breakdown and suicide attempt in 1953 Sylvia Plath was doing research for an honor's thesis on twins in the works of James Joyce; she eventually wrote her thesis on the double in Dostoevski. And she was interested in witchcraft, the occult, astrology, and the like, traditions which at many times and in many places have taught that the body is the coffin of a spirit fed by chthonic energies. But her opposed characters have also a personal reference and source. They carry with them into the prose and poetry contours of the persons, incidents, and landscapes amidst which they were formed, no matter what the distorting pressure of the new contexts. The opposed characters are each associated with a separate cluster of attendant persons, incidents, and landscapes; they are associated with successive periods of Sylvia Plath's life. A closer look at the separate worlds of old yellow and the plaster saint may tell us something about what the opposed forces in Sylvia Plath meant to her and what they may mean to us; it may also tell us something about why we read the poetry and why we brood over her life.

At the age of fifteen, Otto Plath emigrated to the United States from Grabow in the Polish Corridor. "My German-speaking father," says Esther Greenwood, heroine of Sylvia Plath's autobiographical novel, *The Bell Jar*, "came from some manic-depressive hamlet in the black heart of Prussia." He became a professor of biology at Boston University, an expert in insects, especially bees, a fact commemorated in a series of poems by his daughter, who commemorated the fact further by keeping bees herself after moving to Devon in 1961. He also taught German. In a poem, Sylvia Plath remembers his voice as "Gothic and barbarous, pure German"; and the one subject in college Esther Greenwood cannot master, although, like her author, she is a great getter of straight A's, is German: "the very sight of those dense, barbed-wire letters made my mind shut like a clam." While studying for an M.A. in German, Aurelia Schrober, born of Austrian parents, met her husband-to-be.

Their daughter was born on October 27, 1932, and spent the first eight or nine years of her life in the sea-shore town of Winthrop, Massachusetts; but she was frequently a guest at the home of her maternal grandparents at Point Shirley, where the sea is on one side and the bay on the other. Point Shirley, and "the beautiful form-lessness of the sea" around it, appears more often than any other landscape in Sylvia Plath's poetry and prose. In an autobiographical essay, "OCEAN 1212-W," which gets its title from her grandparents' phone number, she begins by explaining that "My childhood landscape was not land but the end of the land—the cold, salt running hills of the Atlantic. I sometimes think my vision of the sea is the clearest thing I own." In her recollection, at least, her fascination with the sea began quite early: "When I was learning to creep, my mother set me down on the beach to see what I thought of it. I crawled straight for the coming wave and was just through the wall of green when she caught my heels." What would have happened, she wonders, "if I had managed to pierce that looking-glass?"

She goes on to describe how when she was two and one-half years old, on the day her brother was born, she walked along the beach and saw for the first time "the *separateness* of everything. I felt the wall of my skin: I am I. That stone is a stone. My beautiful fusion with the things of this world was over." On this day, the "awful birthday of otherness," she became "my rival, somebody else." When her mother read to her from Matthew Arnold's "The Forsaken Merman," she felt shaken, as by a chill; the gooseflesh rose; she wanted to cry: "I had fallen into a new way of being happy." And on the day she suffered the awful birthday of otherness, she looked to the sea for "a sign of election and special-ness." The sea threw up to her a forsaken merman of sorts, a "totem," a carved, wooden sacred baboon: "So the sea, perceiving my need, had conferred a blessing." This account strikes me as more parable than history, its truth more imaginative than literal. It is a myth whose incidents and images express how the sea had come to saturate her sense of identity as well as her sense of being her rival, somebody else, and how the sea had come to represent for her the depths of poetry, in which literal losses underwent a change into symbolic recoveries. "OCEAN 1212-W" ends with these words: "And this is how it stiffens, my visions of that seaside childhood. My father died, we moved inland. Whereon those nine first years of my life sealed themselves off like a ship in a bottle—beautiful, inaccessible, obsolete, a fine, white flying myth."

70

A week after her eighth birthday, her father died, she moved inland, her childhood sealed itself off, in something like a bell jar, inaccessible except as myth. "After that," says Esther Greenwood, whose experiences are a pointed version of her author's, "I had never been happy again"—not since "I was about nine and running along the hot white beaches with my father the summer before he died." He died, in fact, after a long illness, but in the myth a mature Sylvia Plath created of her childhood he becomes a victim of suicide or murder (in each case usually by drowning), or both at once:

I am the ghost of an infamous suicide,
My own blue razor rusting in my throat.
Oh pardon the one who knocks for pardon at
Your gate, father—your hound-bitch, daughter, friend.
It was my love that did us both to death.

These lines are quoted from "Electra on the Azalea Path"; in other poems old yellow speaks out to her "Father, bridegroom" as Clytemnestra raging how she loves and hates him, how she killed him and how he is killing her.

Her own explanation of her love and her hate is one that any amateur Freudian might give. To Nancy Hunter Steiner she said, "He was an autocrat. I adored and despised him, and I probably wished many times that he were dead. When he obliged me and died, I imagined that I had killed him." And so "I Dream that I am Oedipus":

What I want back is what I was
Before the bed, before the knife,
Before the brooch-pin and salve
Fixed me in this parenthesis.

71

She is fixed in a parenthesis because she is sealed off from her childhood—"O I am too big to go backward"—and because in the only future she can imagine her father rises from the waters of her past:

The future is a grey seagull
Tattling in its cat-voice of departure, departure.
Age and terror, like nurses, attend her,
And a drowned man, complaining of the great cold,
Crawls up out of the sea.

Even when she longs for death, for "the black amnesias of heaven," when she thinks of getting "through to a heaven/Starless and fatherless, a dark water," the heaven is black, her father's color, and it is a dark water, her father's element. Fixed in this parenthesis, all she can do is

walk dry on your kingdom's border
Exiled to no good.

Your shelled bed I remember.
Father, this thick air is murderous.
I would breathe water.

Whether Laius, Agamemnon, Proteus, a colossus, a vampire, or murdered god, always, "This is the tongue of the dead man: remember, remember" and always,

It is a chilly god, a god of shades,
Rises to the glass from his black fathoms.

In his essay on the uncanny, Freud argued that the apparitions of a subconscious wish, as in a dream, say, or in hallucination or a work of art, are distorted by the disapproving superego into malevolent and sinister shapes that threaten with what they promise, that insinuate the desire beneath the fear. The superego turns into a source of revulsion what the subconscious finds attractive. But the case of Sylvia Plath is all the more unsettling in that neither the attraction nor the revulsion is subconscious. She knows perfectly well that what her submerged self wants the plaster saint disapproves of, and she knows why, too. No matter how deep her self-analysis, no matter how great her self-knowledge, and it was very great, the black, watery, malevolent, timeless world of raging, lustful, childish old yellow remained the *thesis* of her poetry and of the dialectic that shaped her life, as she understood it. To the antithesis we now turn.

Within a few months of her father's death, Sylvia Plath published her first poem (in the Boston *Sunday Herald*) and her first drawing, for which she won a prize. Those perfect report cards began coming in, with always an "A," a "100," an "excellent" after every subject, including deportment. There followed an unbroken string of awards, prizes, scholarships, elections to honor societies —the goads and lures for what are now called aggressive achievers. No doubt this inexorable academic success was encouraged by a mother who had become a school-teacher, who had wanted to be a professor, and who was making many sacrifices to ensure that her daughter's life would be less restricted than her own, less dependent upon men. Says Esther Greenwood, "My mother had taught shorthand and typing to support us ever since my father died and secretly she hated it and hated him for dying and leaving no money because he didn't trust life-insurance salesmen." Listening to her mother's stories about her marriage, Esther Greenwood comes to feel that being a wife was "like being brainwashed, and afterward you went about numb as a slave in some private, totalitarian state." She decides that she "hates the idea of serving men in any way," and as for the consequences of serving men—"children made me sick."

Such passages led one critic to praise *The Bell Jar* as a chronicle of "genuinely feminist aspirations." They have led some feminists to find in Sylvia Plath a heroine and others to find in the course of her life a cautionary tale with a moral. Germaine Greer, for example, has claimed that if the new feminists had been around in 1963, Sylvia Plath would not have had to commit suicide. The claim seems excessive. Certainly Sylvia Plath did not herself see the demons that attended her as vengeful spirits conjured up by the social status of women. And she attributes Esther Greenwood's attitudes toward men, marriage, and children to the bad air inside the bell jar of neurosis.

Poems such as "Lesbos" suggest that she would not have liked Women's Liberation and that she did not like the feminist streak, such as it was, in herself. She wrote to friends that she married Ted Hughes in part because "He was very simply the only man I've ever met whom I could never boss." She turned out to be an exceptional cook, an efficient housekeeper, and a loving mother. The attitudes toward men most persistently expressed in her writing, rather than comprising a spinsterish resentment or a feminist demand for justice, add up to something more like the female equivalent of misogyny, which is not male chauvinism, but the outcome of a need and a longing so urgent and so fantastic that no living woman can satisfy it. The size of a misogynist's hatred of women is equal to the distance between the compliant creatures of his fantasies, who exist only to gratify him, and actual women, who exist in their own right. And yet living women remind him of his fantasies more than anything else. So it seems to me with Sylvia Plath's misandry. For one thing, no living man could measure up to the colossus that bestrode the fantasy world of her childhood, dripping salt water. And yet it was only living men who partook of his quality, no matter how far they fell short. Because she understood all this, and because she had no gift for evasion, she could not lull herself into that daydream first worked out by Charlotte Brontë, whose situation was similar, and since reworked by a host of imitators: in Sylvia Plath's writing there is no Rochester—no hawk-nosed, piercing-eyed, awesome father/lover is turned into a doting and diminished husband/child. The longing and the hate remain, unresolved, and assume in the poetry the lustful and avenging shapes of vampires, witches, and Medusa.

Sylvia Plath's mother, then, in the poems and in *The Bell Jar*, is associated with the antithetical go-getter's plaster saint of a self, that stiff, driven, and spinsterish achiever of goals set for her by other people. It is probably no confusion of art and life to say that she was unfair to her mother, as she was unfair to her father, who after all did not die just to make his daughter miserable.

During the late forties and early fifties the prevailing winds of opinion were especially such as to confirm and accelerate the tendency of any teenager who began with private reasons for becoming a dissatisfied satisfier of other people's expectations.

She became, said Sylvia Plath, "a rabid teenage pragmatist." The rabidity, which turned the pragmatism into something else, was unusual, but the pragmatism was not. The social pseudosciences, for example, were pragmatical as can be. They advertised the notion that all people at all times and in all places inevitably conform in one way or another to the mores that define the societies in which they live. Whether inner-, outer-, or other-directed, you are directed to defer private inclinations to the public welfare, upon which your own depends. Utopia had never been, nor would be, so the argument ran; there were certain minor injustices in the United States, and a certain amount of inefficiency, as was bound to be the case in a democracy. But if your antennae were sensitive, if you learned the rules, if you did in public what "society" required of you for its own well being, "society" would reciprocate with material compensations and with an unprecedented freedom to do whatever you wanted in private. The concrete application of these lessons, among the representative men who graduated from college in 1955, the year of Sylvia Plath's graduation (and my own), was to look for a job with a large corporation, so that if you were careful not to wear brown socks with a blue suit during the weekdays, you were allowed and could afford to spend the weekends behind your curtained picture windows, watching dirty movies. Representative women looked for such men to marry. As

Sylvia Plath wrote of that period, "The Times Are Tidy":

> There's no career in the venture
> Of riding against the lizard,
> Himself withered these latter-days
> To leaf-size from lack of action:
> History's beaten the hazard.

We get a sense of how well she learned the lessons of her tidy times, and how thoroughly her rabid pragmatism applied them, from a summary by Lois Ames (from whose excellent biographical essays* I have taken many facts and quotations) of Plath's high school years:

> She played tennis, was on the girls' basketball team, was co-editor of the school newspaper, *The Bradford*, joined a high school sorority, Sub-Debs, painted decorations for class dances, went on college weekend dates, was Lady Agatha in the class play, *The Admirable Crichton*,

and got terrific grades. At Smith, Nancy Hunter Steiner reports, the majority opinion was that, except for the intelligence and the poetry, Plath "could have been an airline stewardess or the ingenuous heroine of a B movie." Robert Lowell, who met her a few years later, noted "the checks and courtesies" of a laborious shyness, "an air of maddening docility." And A. Alvarez, who met her a

* "Notes Toward a Biography" in *The Art of Sylvia Plath*, Charles Newman, ed. (Bloomington: Indiana University Press, Midland Paperback, 1971), pp. 155-173; and "Sylvia Plath: A Biographical Note" in *The Bell Jar*, Sylvia Plath (New York: Harper & Row, Inc., 1971).

few years later still, noted "That curious, advertisement-trained, transatlantic air of anxious pleasantness." Pragmatically perhaps, but rabidly for certain, she was "Adhering to rules, to rules, to rules." She was, she came to feel, as though dead, but

> unbothered by it,
> Staying put according to habit.

The social cast of her personality, anesthetic, frozen in a cover-girl smile, mother-directed rather than father-haunted, historical and local rather than mythographic, pragmatic in its protective coloring but rabid in its need for such coloring, fiercely self-denying and self-controlled, anxious, up-tight, and doomed, seems to have remained in charge during her first three years at Smith College, where she continued to do what you were supposed to do, only better than anyone else, and where she wrote stories and poems that were published in *Seventeen*, *The Christian Science Monitor*, *Mademoiselle*, and *Harper's Magazine*. In the summer of 1953 she was chosen to serve as a guest editor for *Mademoiselle*. Her scrapbook description of that month in New York would be funny if it had come from a character in a novel by, for example, Mary McCarthy, but coming from Sylvia Plath it is both sad and infuriating. The accents are those of the American Girl as we want her; it is infuriating that we want her that way, as it is infuriating and sad that Sylvia Plath was so anxious to comply with what we want:

> I won a guest editorship representing Smith & took a train to NYC for a salaried month working—hatted & heeled—in Mlle's airconditioned Madison Ave. offices. . . . Fantastic, fabulous, and all other

inadequate adjectives go to describe the four gala
and chaotic weeks I worked as guest managing Ed ...
living in luxury at the Barbizon, I edited, met celeb-
rities, was fêted and feasted by a galaxy of UN dele-
gates, simultaneous interpreters & artists . . . this
Smith Cinderella met idols: Vance Bourjaily, Paul
Engle, Elizabeth Bowen—wrote articles via cor-
respondence with 5 handsome young male poet
teachers.

The Bell Jar gives us some idea of what old yellow was
doing while the Smith Cinderella was fêted and feasted
by a galaxy of idols. It was emerging through the cracks
that opened all over the plaster saint from the shock of
its collision with New York City. In New York, Plath
ran smack into the reality principle, as though it had been
lurking in ambush to exact revenge for having been so
long and so relentlessly denied. She had knocked into
her how little she would be prepared upon graduation to
make her way in New York as an editor and writer. "I
felt terribly inadequate," says Esther Greenwood. "The
trouble was I had been inadequate all along, I simply
hadn't thought about it. The one thing I was good at was
winning scholarships and prizes and that era was coming
to an end." She feels her carefully built up public personality dissolve as, she says, "all the little successes I'd
trotted up so happily at college fizzled to nothing outside
the slick marble and plate-glass fronts along Madison
Avenue." Above all, her Betty Coed prudishness found
itself squeezed between the lusts and kinks of New York
swingers from without and her own awakening sexuality
from within.

"When I was nineteen, pureness was the great issue," says Esther Greenwood. From a poem ("Fever 103°"), old yellow answers: "Pure? What does it mean?" Wedged, for the time, between countervailing forces of equal potency, Esther Greenwood can move neither way:

> . . . I wondered why I couldn't go the whole way doing what I should any more. This made me sad and tired. Then I wondered why I couldn't go the whole way doing what I shouldn't, . . . and this made me even sadder and more tired.

But old yellow begins to break through "yellower than ever," takes charge, decides to seduce a simultaneous interpreter from the U.N., fails, and, according to the logic of such things, suffers in return a beating and attempted rape, in a patch of black mud, by a South American playboy woman-hater, who acts as though he knew what secretly she was after. "Slut!" he says: "Your dress is black and the dirt is black as well." She leaves New York to return to her home and her mother, but that whole life now seems "vacuous." She goes, for the first time, to her father's grave: "I laid my face to the smooth face of the marble and howled my loss into the cold salt rain." The next morning she squeezes into the crawl space beneath her house, where "a dim, undersea light filtered through the slits of the cellar windows." She wraps her black raincoat around her "like my own sweet shadow," and swallows, one by one, a bottle of sleeping pills: "The silence drew off, baring the pebbles and shells and all the tatty wreckage of my life. Then, at the rim of vision, it gathered itself, and in one sweeping tide, rushed me to sleep."

That sea imagery and an enveloping blackness accompany old yellow's return to her element is what we might expect. Sylvia Plath herself understood the suicide attempt as an effort to rejoin her father, to appear before him free from the tight, but life-preserving, social self she had wrapped herself in, pure once more:

> And I, stepping from this skin
> Of old bandages, boredoms, old faces
>
> Step to you from the black car of Lethe,
> Pure as a baby.

The suicide attempt of 1953, however, did not succeed. She was found, hospitalized, and subjected to a course of therapy that included treatments of electric shock. By midwinter she was back at Smith, "Facing & reconstructing the old wrecked life—new & strong." And at the end of the term, the false, flat, bright, insistent voice of the go-getter is back in the scrapbook to claim that "exams & papers proved I hadn't lost either my repetitive or my creative intellect as I had feared . . . a semester of reconstruction ends with an infinitely more solid if less flashingly spectacular flourish than last year's." But Nancy Hunter Steiner's *A Closer Look at Ariel*, the closest and most clear-eyed look at Sylvia Plath we have, tells us that the reconstructed "typical American girl, the product of a hundred years of middle-class propriety," was suffering from something like ontological insecurity. She hangs on, as though for life, to the material possessions that constitute the visible reaches of her reconstructed identity. She is roused to a shrill passion when another girl merely observes that their hairdos are the same. She would have felt "raped intellectually," as she puts it, had anyone disturbed the finicky arrangement of her dresser drawers. She sets up little melodramas to test the loyalty of her friends. And at the same time, old yellow, "the blond bitch," as she is called by the wife of a Harvard professor, becomes yellower and yellower, reveals a special interest in older men, especially professors, and gets herself raped by the sinister and repulsive Irwin, professor of biology.

A Closer Look at Ariel, besides giving us the most vivid and most understanding account we have of how the opposed twin poles that charge Sylvia Plath's writing alternated in the currents of her life, also gives some insight into how she reshaped the life to heighten the significance and tighten the forms of the writings. In the novel, as distinct from the life, the Irwin affair and its consequences neatly conclude the old life that the fictional heroine, as distinct from the real woman, sloughed off and left behind. Esther Greenwood's best friend at the time is Joan Gilling, who insists on accompanying a cool Esther to the doctor when Irwin's rape causes her to hemorrhage, but Sylvia Plath hysterically would not allow Nancy Hunter to leave her for a minute. She tells us that Sylvia Plath "referred to me in letters to her mother as her alter ego and often remarked that we presented a mirror image or represented opposite sides of the same coin." Esther Greenwood tells us that "sometimes I wondered if I had made Joan up." Of herself and Joan she says, "we were close enough so that her thoughts and feelings seemed a wry, black image of my own." But Joan is entirely different from Mrs. Steiner in physical appearance, character, and personal background. Joan is a childhood friend, a constant reminder to Esther "of what I had been, and what I had been through"; she had wanted to marry the suitor whom Esther rejects; she especially loves the suitor's family, which Esther Greenwood scorns, unlike Sylvia Plath, who described in her scrapbook the family of the young man on whom the suitor is modeled as her ideal. Joan turns out to be a lesbian. When Joan commits suicide, right after and partially in reaction to Esther's hemorrhaging, Esther feels the bell jar lift; she decides for life; she feels that a surrogate self had died so that she might live, whereas Nancy Hunter is forced to put some distance between herself and Sylvia Plath so that she might continue to live her own life, rather than serve as a portion of her friend's. It is clear that Joan's character is a kind of disposal unit for traits that Sylvia Plath came to reject in herself. Mrs. Steiner was nothing of the sort, although it is also clear she would have been just that had Sylvia Plath gotten her way. To the extent that she did get her way Nancy Hunter was cast in the role of the plaster saint, so that Sylvia Plath might be free to play old yellow with a single mind.

A Closer Look at Ariel, then, tells us much about Sylvia Plath of which we would otherwise have no inkling and about much that other sources only imply, such as the hypochondriacal fear and fascination with which she regarded the functions and malfunctions of her own body. One is especially grateful for the episodes of mundane happiness, as on the giggly afternoon when Miss Plath and Miss Hunter sat white-gloved in the cavernous parlor of Olive Higgins Prouty, devouring platters of cucumber sandwiches under the disdainful eye of a cartoon butler. For its intelligence, its sense of the historical moment, its clear-eyed sympathy, tact, and narrative pace, the memoir would be worth reading, even if it were about some anonymous college girl of the fifties, even if it were a piece of fiction, rather than the best-informed account we are likely to have of crucial events in the life and art of an important poet and notorious suicide.

There were occasions enough for more than mundane happiness in the eight years or so Sylvia Plath lived after she and Nancy Hunter went their separate ways. The prizes and fellowships continued to come. The poems also continued to come, and as time went on they came easier; good as they had been, they got better. They were accepted for publication in many journals. *The Colossus* and *The Bell Jar* were favorably reviewed, for the most part. She married a man she could respect as well as love. She traveled—"so much! the whole world coming alive, banging through my eyes and fibers!" She returned to Smith as an instructor, triumphantly successful in the role of "triple-threat woman: wife, writer & teacher (to be swapped later for motherhood, I hope)," as she described her aspiration. After she swapped teaching for motherhood she seems to have felt, sometimes at least, that her children rounded her completeness, that they demonstrated to herself and to the world how the squint-eyed poet was also a golden girl. Ted Hughes describes the births of the two children as crucial stages in his wife's movement toward self-acceptance.

She even seems for a time to have found formulas for exorcizing the ugly and hairy underside of her personality, for converting the blasting furies into bountiful eumenides. Freud explains in *Beyond the Pleasure Principle* and in a number of essays how in play, in dreams, or in art, we may mime the ghosts of traumas that hold us in thrall. We may confront or manipulate in play, or dreams, or art the representation of what in life was or is traumatically unbearable so that it becomes familiar, domestic, bearable, a source, even, of aesthetic pleasure. Plath's note on "Daddy," written for a BBC audience, is Freudian in this sense, among others:

> The poem is spoken by a girl with an Electra Complex. Her case is complicated by the fact that her father was also a Nazi and her mother very possibly part Jewish. In the daughter the two strains marry and paralyze each other—she has to act out the awful little allegory once over before she is free of it.

In the same exorcizing mood she wrote *The Bell Jar*, which she described as "an autobiographical apprentice work which I had to write in order to free myself from the past."

And while she was trying to free herself from the traumas of her past by discharging them into the forms of her art, she and her husband "devised exercises of meditation and invocation," as he tells us, to help her "break down the tyranny, the fixed focus and the public persona which descriptive or discursive poems take as a norm" and to help her "accept the invitation of her inner world." That she accepted that invitation the poems written in the last two years of her life and *The Bell Jar* testify well enough. A number of passages celebrate the exhilarating sense of release that sometimes accompanied the breakdown of the fixed focus and the public persona. In the novel, for example, Esther Greenwood's one moment of unqualified happiness occurs when on skis she doesn't know how to use she schusses down a slope:

> I felt my lungs inflate with the inrush of scenery—air, mountains, trees, people. I thought, "This is what it is to be happy."
> I plummeted down past the zigzaggers, the students, the experts, through year after year of doubleness and smiles and compromise, into my own past.

Similarly in "Years" she writes that

> What I love is
> The piston in motion—
> My soul dies before it.
> And the hooves of the horses,
> Their merciless churn.

In "Stings" she has "a self to recover, a queen," a queen bee, whose wings, like the hooves of her horse Ariel, rush her past the boundaries of selfhood into new dimensions:

> Now she is flying
> More terrible than she ever was, red
> Scar in the sky, red comet
> Over the engine that killed her—
> The mausoleum, the wax house.

But in other poems, the crumbling of the public persona and the solicitations of the inner world are experienced not with exhilaration, as a soaring release after long confinement, but with anxiety and dread, with a sense of being in the grips of an implacable force riding her irresistibly to no good end:

> the wind
> Pours by like destiny, bending
> Everything in one direction.

Then the pistons shriek and the hoofbeats appall:

> The train is dragging itself, it is screaming—
> An animal
> Insane for the destination,
> The bloodspot,
> The face at the end of the flare.

The ego is reduced to numb helplessness by the solicitations of the ghosts it called up but cannot control—"the dead injure me with attentions, and nothing can happen." It stands helpless before its own dissolution:

> See, the darkness is leaking from the cracks.
> I cannot contain it. I cannot contain my life.

In the winter of 1962-1963, the coldest in a century, the dread and depression found allies against the exhilaration. She was cold, ill, lonely, separated from her husband, unable to sleep. More than ever, as Ted Hughes said, "She had none of the usual guards and remote controls to protect herself from her own reality." Once again, death began to impend like "A Birthday Present," a promise of a condition in which "split lives congeal and stiffen to history." When A. Alvarez visited her near Christmas, her hair, the exclusive styling of which had formed part of her reconstructed identity and which she later wore in a finicky bun, hung loose down to her waist and gave off "a strong smell, sharp as an animal's." Six weeks later she killed herself.

> From the bottom of a pool, fixed stars
> Govern a life.

GEORGE STADE

September, 1972
Columbia University